In this WMG Writer's Guide, *USA Today* bestselling author and former publisher Dean Wesley Smith addresses the ten most damaging myths that writers believe about indie publishing.

The
WMG Writer's Guide
Series

KILLING

THE TOP 10

Sacred Cows

OF Indie PUBLISHING

A WMG WRITER'S GUIDE

DEAN WESLEY SMITH

wmg PUBLISHING

Killing the Top Ten Sacred Cows of Indie Publishing

Published 2014 by WMG Publishing
www.wmgpublishing.com
Cover art © copyright Robyn Mackenzie/Dreamstime
Book and cover design copyright © 2014 WMG Publishing
Cover design by Allyson Longueira/WMG Publishing
ISBN-13: 978-1-56146-612-2
ISBN-10: 1-56146-612-3

First published in slightly different form on Dean Wesley Smith's blog at www.deanwesleysmith.com in 2014.

For all the brave writers out there who are going it alone.
Have fun.

Contents

KILLING
THE **TOP 10**
Sacred Cows
Indie
OF PUBLISHING

A WMG WRITER'S GUIDE

INTRODUCTION

Welcome to the second book in the Killing the Sacred Cows series. The first book was called simply, *Killing the Top Ten Sacred Cows of Publishing.*

Both books are about the myths, which I call "Sacred Cows," that infest the publishing industry. I've been writing about these myths, killing one sacred cow after another, on my web site for years now.

Finally, last year, some of the readers convinced me I needed to put the Sacred Cows into a book. So I took what I thought were the top ten myths about publishing in general and created the first book.

But then, as the indie publishing world started to grow and gain traction, it became clear to me that the writers thinking of indie publishing were getting pounded with a lot of myths as well.

So thus this second book.

All the chapters in the two books were blog posts on my website and have some wonderful comments and questions attached. So feel free to go follow the discussions and ask questions.

There is a tab at the top of my website called Killing Sacred Cows that links to all the different chapters in a rougher form.

Why I Can Write About This Stuff

I sold my first short story in 1975, and have been pushing and working at writing ever since. I went through many of the general myths from the first book and survived them and finally started making a living in publishing in 1987, the same year I sold my first novel.

Also that year, Kristine Kathryn Rusch and I started a publishing company called Pulphouse Publishing, which quickly grew to be the fifth largest publisher of science fiction, fantasy, and horror in the nation.

I was the publisher and sometimes editor on some projects.

We shut the business down in 1996, but I kept editing at times, first for a magazine, then for Pocket Books in the *Star Trek* department. Also, during that time and up until around 2008, I sold over one hundred novels under various names to traditional publishers.

So sitting in the writer desk, the editor desk, and the publisher desk allowed me to see all sides of this business. And working for such a long time writing many, many novels, helped me clear out the last of the myths for myself.

Then the indie revolution started and I loved it right off.

I loved the freedom and the fact that I didn't have to spend so much time dealing with editors and such in New York.

So in 2009, Kris and I once again started up a publishing company called WMG Publishing Inc. to work on our indie titles and get our backlist out.

Now, as I write this in 2014, WMG Publishing Inc. has seven employees and three more coming on in the fall. It has over

400 titles in print and is publishing not only Kris's work and my work, but work by a lot of other writers as well.

So I know the indie side as well as the traditional side.

And both Kris and I have been voices in the indie growth on our blogs since it started.

The Goal of This Book

Writers hold onto myths like lifelines that are keeping them from drowning in a raging river of information. Sometimes sane people in the normal world will follow a publishing myth that makes no sense at all.

And they follow the myth, the sacred cow, without thought.

So this new series is an attempt to help the new world of indie publishing with the growing list of myths that plague it.

My goal is simply to show other sides of myths, to help writers become grounded in good business decisions.

Writing fiction is a business. Indie publishing your fiction is a business.

This indie publishing business can be fantastic fun and very profitable if you can make clear business decisions that are right for you.

My goal is to not show you the right way, or the only way, or any other such nonsense.

My goal is to help you push aside the myths that are swirling around publishing and make good decisions for yourself.

Thanks for reading. I hope this book helps your writing and publishing dreams in some fashion or another.

—Dean Wesley Smith
June 9th, 2014
Lincoln City, Oregon

Sacred Cow #1

YOU CAN'T GET YOUR BOOKS INTO BOOKSTORES

Or put more clearly,

INDIE WRITERS CAN'T GET THEIR BOOKS INTO BOOKSTORES

Fact: Of course indie writers/publishers can. But some things must be done correctly and the bookstore owners or buyers must know your book is there. And it also must be something that fits what they are selling.

I'll lay it out below and in even more detail in a lecture that is now available under the lecture tab called "How to Get Your Books into Bookstores."

But let me say this here. Traditional publishers don't have magic wands that ship their books into bookstores. They simply know how to do it and indie publishers have yet to learn. Or at least some indie publishers. Some of us already know how and are making great money on paper books.

First Some History

As with all these publishing myths, to really grasp the myth and get past it, an indie publisher must know where the myth came from and why there used to be a little truth to the myth. Not much, but a little. Myths in publishing are often formed from half-truths of the past. But just as if you don't need a buggy whip to start your car, you don't need an agent to sell a book, or a traditional publisher to make a living at fiction writing.

And traditional publishers can't magically block you from going into bookstores. They can't even try, to be honest.

So where did this myth start? Most of it came from the old days of warehouse publishing and vanity press publishing. Writers (often horrid writers, but not all) would spend thousands and thousands of dollars through a scam vanity press to get a garage full of really ugly books. Then these poor writers would wander the roads and the streets peddling their books to any unsuspecting store who let them in the door.

Store owners hated these vanity-press people almost as much as they hated a young traditionally published writer with a handful of bookmarks. Sometimes a vanity press book had a local interest and the bookstore owner would take a few. (Young writers with bookmarks who demanded to have a signing were just flat annoying.)

Also, in those vanity press days, traditional publishers seemed to have a stranglehold on the book distribution network.

Of course, that wasn't true either, but it **seemed** that way.

In 1987, Kris and I started an indie publisher (called a small press back then) named Pulphouse Publishing. We got our books and magazines into traditional distribution systems just fine. Our magazines were on newsstands. And the company lasted for nine years selling to bookstores. Go figure.

Why could we do it? Simple, actually. We spent the little bit of time and energy to learn how to slot our books into what are called "the trade distribution systems." No one in the distribution system seemed to care that Pulphouse wasn't in New York City. Or that when we started we only had two books our first year.

Some Terms Before Moving Forward

POD means Print on Demand printing. Createspace, LightningSource, and others are *printers*, not publishers. You (your publishing business name) is the publisher.

DISTRIBUTORS are the companies that take your book from one place and sell them to another place. Baker & Taylor and Ingrams are two of the biggest distributors. There are thousands of smaller distributors that function in many areas, from regional to gift shops to books only on a certain topic. You name it, there's a distributor for it.

BOOKSTORES are places that sell your books to readers. Susy's Local Gift and Bookshop is a bookstore. Amazon is a bookstore. Kobo is a bookstore.

INDIE BOOKSTORE is a bookstore that is not associated with a chain store, or Amazon. Indie bookstores can be a chain, so the line is pretty vague most of the time. Powell's Bookstore based in Portland is considered an indie store, but it is owned by a corporation and has many stores and a major online web selling site. Go figure.

ABA is the American Booksellers Association, a group made up of bookstores and publishers. (Yes, you can join as a publisher for around $300 bucks, give or take.) Their focus is to help bookstores learn new methods of selling and be a connection between publishers and bookstores. The ABA has many, many programs that help bookstores discover new books coming out. Some indie publishers can get into the programs, some a new indie publisher can't get into.

INDIE PUBLISHER. A writer or group of writers who have a real publishing name and imprint and act like a business using a business imprint name such as Teddy Press or CAT Publishing.

SELF-PUBLISHED WRITER. A writer who publishes under his or her own name, with no business publishing name. This will block you from most bookstores I'm afraid. (If you don't know how to get a business name, read my "Think Like a Publisher" articles under the tab above. It's scary simple.)

So What Has Changed in the Last Ten Years?

When looked at in cold, hard terms, not much I'm afraid. I know those of you with no sense of history in publishing will scream at that, but sadly, it's the truth.

The real question, as Passive Guy has continually pointed out, is what will the disruptive technology hitting publishing change in the future. The big change has yet to come. And from what I can see, legacy (or big traditional) publishing is not reacting well so far.

So what hasn't changed? Let's look at history.

Pulp magazines came in around the last part of the 1800s and changed distribution of novels and stories to readers.

Then in the late 1930s, but mostly into the late 1940s, mass market paperbacks came in and changed distribution of novels and stories to readers.

And electronic books have now done exactly the same thing once again starting in 2009.

Nothing new, just the standard cycle of a new form of distribution of novels and stories to readers coming in. These changes tend to happen to allow overpriced books to find a less-expensive way to the general public. Pulps did that around 1900 and paperbacks did that in 1950 and now, sixty years later, history repeats yet again.

For those of you who are history challenged, the articles you see about what electronic books are doing are almost word-for-word from articles done about the advent of pulps. And word-for-word about the advent of the mass market paperback.

And those of you who don't like Amazon, they own very, very little of the sales market compared to the old *American News Company*, that basically controlled all magazine, most comics, and most book distribution in this country in the first half of last century. Then one day in 1957 they just shut their doors.

By the height of the pulps in 1940, about 50% of all novels published were only published in the pulps. In the height of the mass market paperbacks, around 2005, about 50% of all novels published were only published in mass market paperbacks. It's a safe bet that will be the number for electronic novels as well in a decade or so.

History can teach us a lot in publishing.

But how about indie publishing? That's new, right? We're all out in the great unknown, right?

Uhhh, no. Writers were publishing their own books for a very long time before "Vanity Press" scams made it a bad thing in the 1950s. Before the 1950s, publishing your own work or starting your own press was an accepted part of publishing. And the list of authors from that century who self-published their own books could fill a large book in very tiny print. It was perfectly accepted, as it is becoming yet again.

Nothing new. Goes around, comes around, and all that.

Let me give you just one minor example. Arkham House, run by August Derelith, the writer, started to reprint a few Lovecraft works. But almost half of all Arkham House books for the first thirty years were Derelith books. You really would have fun studying the real history behind some of the major traditional presses now and how they got started and why. Like Simon and Sons.

And folks, if you really go back and look at old books from a hundred years ago, you will see almost no sign, if any, of the publishers of today. The publishers you all think of as huge now were small press or solo shops, indie presses, back 50 or 100 years ago. The indie presses grew up to replace the old, slow legacy publishers of that day. And that's what is happening now as well.

In 1987, Kris and I started an indie press. And many small indie presses came and went while we were in business, and I still collect books from some indie presses in the 1950s and 1960s. (Arkham House shut down in 2005, lasting from 1938.)

In other words, there is nothing new happening.

Except... No, let me make that **EXCEPT!!!!!!**

—More people now think they can do it, and thus more people are starting their own publishing companies.

That will have an impact. The full type of impact is yet to be known. Too early.

But with more people doing this, discoverability is a growing problem area that Kris is talking about now in her great blog.

Is this discoverability problem actually new? No, not really once again. The results of books not easily found is that this trend is returning publishing to a time where blockbusters didn't exist. (Yes, I know... but the modern "blockbuster novel" that supports most of traditional publishing didn't really come around until the late 1960s and early 1970s and didn't become part of the traditional publishing business plan until the 1980s.)

So even this flattening of sales across more products has happened before.

I personally think it's a healthy correction, but I haven't been getting millions per book in advances.

So more writers jumping into the mix as indie publishers is the one thing that is different from any time in history. At no time in history have so many writers in such a concerted form, moved to indie publish as a mass.

My honest opinion... For a time that might have some interesting consequences, but I kind of doubt any consequence will be very long term, since most indie publishers will drop away given time, leaving, as normal, only the survivors who can adapt and hold on through the technological-impact changes that are coming.

It's Easy, But It's Not

In the second chapter of Killing the Sacred Cows of Indie Publishing, I'm going to deal with the fact that so many people call this indie publishing "easy." It is, but it isn't.

But for the moment, I want to stay focused on the subject of this chapter.

Getting Your Books into Bookstores.

It's easy, but it's not.

Remember that.

What Does It Mean in 2014 to Have Your Book in a Bookstore?

Way back, again looking at history, bookstores were often the publishers as well. (Yeah, I know, publishers have been talking about vertical structures for some time, looking to see if it is possible to produce books and sell to readers at the same time. Harlequin springs to mind.) And Amazon is playing in that area and Barnes & Noble has had their own publishing arm now for decades (I wrote a bunch of books and stories for B&N).

But back then, way back, before this modern era, bookstore catalogs consisted of what books the bookstore itself had printed, what books they were going to print, and what books they had in stock in their store, and maybe a few other books from a few other bookstore/publishers.

(And by the way, Print on Demand [POD] is also not new... it was being done in the 1800s in the backs of bookstores. We did it in 1987 at Pulphouse because we owned our own press. We printed to order, as did old stores a hundred years ahead of us.)

So what about today?

In today's modern bookstores, a book is considered to be "in the store" when...

1) it is on the shelves, or

2) in the bookstore catalog.

So to get your book into a bookstore, it needs to make it to a bookstore catalog or onto a shelf.

If you are dreaming of having a shelf full of just your book or books in a bookstore (like used to happen ten years ago), you need to change that thinking.

Most bookstores don't operate that way anymore.

Ten years ago, a bookstore would order ten copies of a book to sell five. The other five would get destroyed and credited by the publisher to the bookstore. So a publisher would have to print ten copies to sell five, so the five sold had to carry the weight of the costs of the extra books. That was called "Ordering to Stock" among other terms.

Today, smart bookstores "Order to Replace."

Distribution systems have gotten fast, so a bookstore owner will often take only one or two copies of a book, then when one sells, they order to replace it quickly. No returns and a ton safer.

ABA has been teaching bookstores this method for six years now, plus cash register systems and website book-selling design. That's why, for the last five years, there have been more bookstores than the year before. I know, another myth shot about bookstores going away. Head out of the sand, folks. Numbers of bookstores are increasing. Fact.

Using **Ordering to Replace** system, bookstore owners who are smart can get more titles in the same shelf area.

Think about that...

THIS IS A GOOD THING for all authors, because more authors actually have books in physical form in bookstores for readers to find. Instead of ten of the last Patterson, there are two of the Patterson and eight other authors' books in the same shelf space.

That is a good thing for all readers and writers.

Traditional bestselling mega-authors hate this new practice, however, because so much of the old system was based on **books shipped**, not books sold. That's right, big advances were based on having 100,000 books shipped, even if only 30,000 sold. That second number wasn't seen for months and months. The first number caused books to be on major bestseller lists.

But bookstores don't "Order to Stock," they now "Order to Replace." **That's a HUGE CHANGE.** (Nothing really new, just back to the pre-return system days of book selling.)

That's why you hear idiots like Scott Turow going on about how bad this new world is. He would rather return to the old returns system that destroyed five-out-of-ten books produced so his books-shipped numbers could be high. (And it was that old system that caused bookstores to collapse for eleven straight years of fewer and fewer stores, which is where the fewer bookstore myth comes from. Under the new **Order to Replace** system, bookstores are increasing every year and becoming stable.)

Today, in this new system, the returns system is drifting away and is now under 18% standard and still dropping. (Returns hovered between 50% and 55% at one point.) Many large publishers are even offering no-return choices for higher discounts and bookstores are learning to order smarter.

Give us five more years and the returns system will be around 10%, if that. Nothing more than a sales tool as it started off to be in the depression.

So How Do You Get Your Book Into A Bookstore?

Some basics first. All are critical, but most of you will just glaze over these looking for the secret, and these basics are the secret.

So let me be clear here. **The Secret to Getting Your Books into Bookstores** is:

1... Great cover, branded to genre.

2... Great sales blurbs. (Not your plot, sales blurb...if you don't know sales copy writing, learn it.)

3... A publisher name. (Can't be your writer name as publisher. Bookstores will shy away from that just as they were afraid of those authors with a fist-full of bookmarks coming through the door.)

4... A publisher web site. You also need an author web site. Treat your publisher web site like it is Bantam Books.

5... A major dealer/bookstore discount schedule on your publisher web site. You can copy the WMG Publishing discount schedule if you like.

6... Your paper books need to be priced correctly. Easiest way to figure this is go on CreateSpace to their price calculator, put in your trim size, your page count, and then experiment with prices. When the amount you make in the "extended distribution" program is above $2.00, your book is priced correctly.

From the Bookstore Side

So back in Spring of 2013, things changed in the two major distribution companies and most small distributors are following slowly. Ingrams and Baker & Taylor, for the longest time, had code in their monthly catalogs on the books that were produced with a POD printer. And they limited the discounts bookstores could get on POD books.

Then very silently in March and April of 2013, that code vanished.

The reason is simple. POD books have reached a level of quality that is often above a web press printed book quality. POD books could be done faster. And most importantly, major traditional publishers were using POD for short-run books, for second printings, and so on. So by having the code on there, the distributors were hurting their main clients.

So the code vanished. Poof.

What does that mean? Now your paper book, with your publisher imprint on it, is in the same catalog right beside any of the books from the hundreds of imprints from Random/Penguin. And since readers don't buy for publisher, but for author, any indie book was suddenly sitting beside any traditional book in the big discount catalogs.

And playing with the same tools. And the same field of sale.

So bookstores could order your book if they wanted… if the book looked good… if they knew about it… and if the indie publisher had set the price correctly to allow for enough discounts through the chain of custody for a book.

The key, of course, is that the bookstore owner must learn about your book through the normal trade channels. Granted, some store owners are on Goodreads and watch other reader review sites, but most still find their information through the trade channels.

Can an indie publisher get a book into a trade channel?

Of course. No magic keeping you out, honest there isn't.

A trade channel is simply letting the bookstore know the book is coming. For example, the major trade review magazine for bookstores is *Publisher's Weekly*. All bookstores look at it every week and get it for free. So send your books to *Publisher's Weekly* for review. (Act like a publisher. Don't use the paid side of PW and never buy a review anywhere.)

(I talk about all this over six weeks in the Promotions workshop. Both how to sell to readers and how to sell in the trades, and how to do your catalog copy. And more.)

The ABA has a bunch of fairly inexpensive programs so that you can let a thousand bookstores know your book is coming.

You can send things (not bookmarks), AS A PUBLISHER, directly to the bookstore. Bookstore mailing lists are free on the ABA web site.

Does this all take some time and learning? Yes.

As I said. **It's easy, but it's not.**

But chances are if your book has a good cover, a publisher name, a decent price, and is being carried by any standard entry distributor, it's already making its way to bookstores. The owner might not have a copy on the shelf yet, but it might be in the bookstore online catalog.

CreateSpace extended distribution is a service they provide as an entry point distributor. LightningSource (caution with their terms of service) is not only a printer, but can provide standard entry point to distribution channels.

Or you can have your book printed in any number of POD printers, or small presses in your local area and make a deal with an entry-point distributor and get your books out there.

There are hundreds and hundreds of entry point distributors. As a publisher, you will need to figure out what works for you and what is easiest.

It's easy, but it's not.

If you want really easy, just use CreateSpace and their extended distribution. Scary easy. But they are not the only way into the distribution system by a long, long ways. And with any printer and with any entry distributor, they have their drawbacks.

Make decisions as a publisher for yourself. Think like a business person.

I had my own printer in Pulphouse for most projects, for others I used a press only an hour away and a bindery only an hour away. My distribution was also fairly close when we jumped products into the channels. I found being local and close helped me work tighter with the printer and binder.

But the discount the bookstore is getting is wrong...

Sigh... I have to talk about this just to head off the thousand comments and questions on this one topic.

When a bookstore, and indie bookstore, gets books from distributors, the store tends to have only one or two or three major distributors it uses. This is normal. Think about how they only want to pay three bills per month instead of a dozen and you'll understand.

A distributor (both large and regional distributors) sets a basic discount for a bookstore on a number of factors.

1... How much the bookstore orders from the distributor.

2... The bookstore's credit rating.

3... How fast, over time, the bookstore pays its bills.

So a bookstore who only orders a few books from say Baker & Taylor per month, or who doesn't have a good credit rating, or who often pays late, will be sent the bottom (library) catalog.

If you, the indie author, go in there and convince them to try to order your book and they can only get a 20% discount, then chances are that store doesn't order much from that distributor. Or has credit issues. Or pays bills late.

NOT YOUR FAULT, NOTHING YOU CAN DO. WALK AWAY.

Or offer to sell them copies at your publisher discount.

Let me say this again to be clear... All those factors of bookstore discounts, once your book is priced correctly, are out of your control in almost all distribution channels and through all distributors.

And remember, if you have a good publisher web site, bookstores can order from you for up to 50% free shipping on ten assorted books. If you are thinking you don't want to pack books, you need to really think it through. You don't have to. Duh. You drop-ship the books direct from your printer to the store, just as any traditional publisher drop-ships books to bookstores from their printers. (I used to do this with some Pulphouse magazines from my printer in 1990. Nothing new.)

SUMMARY

You must do some things correctly to get bookstores to order your books. Covers, blurbs, correct pricing, and so on. Those are the secrets.

And as a publisher, you must have enough product to make it worth a bookstore's while to order from you.

But even more important, a bookstore needs to know your book exists. And that's the tough part.

Getting your books into bookstores is easy, but it's not.

But you, as an indie publisher, can absolutely get your books sitting right beside any book from any traditional publisher in a bookstore if you want.

There is no magic roadblock.

If you want, and are crazy enough, you can even get your books to Costco. (Go in there next time and notice how many books in Costco are regional presses. If they can do it, so can you, but I'm not talking about how to do it here. If you have to ask, you aren't ready.)

One of the keys is that you, as the publisher of your own indie books, must decide if paper books are worth it, if having your books in store catalogs and on bookstore shelves are worth it.

And that's a business decision only you can make.

WMG Publishing has books in bookstores and has over 200 titles in paper. For example, take a look at a simple search I did for Kristine Kathryn Rusch at Powell's Books, an indie bookstore. http://www.powells.com/s?kw=Kristine+Kathryn+Rusch&class=

Or a simple search of Kristine Kathryn Rusch books in Mysterious Galaxy Bookstore. http://www.mystgalaxy.com/search/apachesolr_search/Kristine%20Kathryn%20Rusch

We didn't approach either store. Yet WMG books are right there with Kris's traditionally published books just fine. We put the books into the system and let the system take care of itself and we are now working slowly to let bookstores know the books are out.

You know the decision we made three years ago. It's clear.

Getting books into bookstores is easy, but it's not.

But it can clearly be done, and anyone who tells you it can't be is just spouting a myth.

Have fun.

Sacred Cow #2

SELF-PUBLISHING
AND INDIE PUBLISHING IS EASY

Truth: It isn't. But it can be done.

It's easier by factors of thousands of headaches in working with agents and publishers. Sure. But it isn't easy when it comes to the amount of work indie and self-published writers have to do to get their books to readers.

But you hear this insulting and often dismissive comment from people everywhere. "Oh, you should indie (self) publish your work."

They say it as if you could indie publish your book in five minutes.

This comment comes from traditional publishers, editors, agents, and traditional writers who have zero idea what an indie (self) publisher does. Or how much work it is to indie publish a book.

These uninformed people say that statement as a toss-off for all kinds of various reasons, often meant to be insulting or dismissive.

And folks, it's about time to kill this myth that indie publishing is easy.

Reality: Here's what these dismissive people are saying. "Oh, you're out of shape…you should run a marathon."

So this second myth is going to be short because, to be honest, it's just so damn silly. But it needs to be addressed up front in this book.

A Quick Look At Both Major Routes for a Novel to Get to Readers

Writer finishes book.

Traditional writer mails book to agent. Nothing happens for six months, or a year if writer is lucky to have something happen that soon other than numbers of rewrites.

Indie writer gives book to a proofreader and must pay the proofreader real money or trade time and energy for services.

Indie book comes back from proofreader in a month. Indie writer must now either design a cover, or hire the cover done, write blurbs for the novel, set up accounts with different stores and printers and distributors. And then do the layout and learn programs to help with that, or hire it all done. And that's after they have at least set up a publishing name and business.

Usually, since most writers are broke, most of this work is done by the writer.

Book comes out to readers in three or four months. Traditional writer is still hoping for a response from an agent, or working on a rewrite for the agent, months (if ever) from the book even making it to an editor's desk.

BUT… I hear people say, traditional writers can be writing while waiting.

And my response is yes, they can, but for what reason? All but romance publishers hate more than two books a year from any writer. Indie writers can write and publish more books in a year (even with all the extra work) than almost all traditional writers can.

So sure, while indie writers are doing all the work to get their books to readers, traditional writers could be waiting or writing, but for no reason. Even if the traditional writer is fast, eventually the traditional publisher will slow them down and their agent will drop them for not writing the correct book, or something even uglier will happen.

That's the nature of the traditional publishing world I'm afraid.

Why is this "Indie is Easy" myth dangerous?

When I hear some agent or editor or traditional writer tell a new writer "Oh, you should self-publish that," I get worried for newer writers.

Or I hear New York people going on and on about how threatened they are by all the writers indie publishing, I get worried for newer writers.

That indie publishing is easy is a myth. NEW WRITERS SUCK UP MYTHS like a sponge sucks up water.

Since New York people have no idea how hard all the indie writers are working, spending their own time, energy, and capital to get their books directly to readers, a writer told that it is easy, or led to believe it is easy, will quickly get discouraged when they try it.

I am already seeing this happen a lot to younger writers, actually.

Not only is the writer giving up the false dream of being stamped with approval from Simon and Schuster, but they are discovering that indie publishing is a lot of work, or very expensive. Or both.

And that turns many people away from writing and their dreams of being a writer. All because they heard people say that indie publishing was easy and it really isn't.

INDIE PUBLISHING CAN BE DONE, but it's not easy. It takes work and learning.

To learn how to indie publish, you must do the following things to start.

1… Follow the steps I lay out in the first and second chapter under the tab above called "Think Like a Publisher" to get your business going. It's simple and easy and cheap.

2… Learn how to do covers well enough to either do them yourself, or know what you are hiring.

3… Learn how to write good sales copy for your books. Not plot, sales copy.

4… Set up all the accounts needed to get your eBooks into as many online stores as you can, which means learning how to do clean ePub files these days.

5… Launch your book to all sites and fight through all that.

6… Learn how to do paper books, or hire it done.

7… And then the promotion starts, which will depend on the amount depending on the book. You have to constantly be learning about promotion and discoverability.

And you have to keep working on being a better storyteller, which is actually what sells books.

Yes, that's a lot of work.

But it can be done. And it can be learned slowly, just as training for a marathon is slow.

So, next time some idiot says to you in some flippant manner, "You should self publish your novel," tell them they should run a marathon in the same tone they used with you.

They could run a marathon, but it won't be easy.

Maybe they will stop saying something so stupid, and by you stopping just one person from passing something so false and misleading, you might save a new writer who will learn that indie publishing is work. And go into it with their eyes open.

Indie (self) publishing can be done. Just as running a marathon can be done.

It's not easy, but it is a ton of fun.

Sacred Cow #3

NO ONE WILL PAY GOOD MONEY FOR AN UNKNOWN WRITER'S WORK

(So a new writer should make his or her work cheaper because it's worth less.)

Thankfully, just a tiny bit of thought will kill this silliness for most people. But it is one of the most repeated myths young writers have.

Some History

Fact: Every writer started off as a new writer. (I know, shock.)

Fact: Every new writer who sold to traditional publishing for the first time in the last hundred years was paid decent, good, or fantastic money. Why? Because the gatekeepers thought they could sell a lot of copies of (you guessed it) an Unknown Writer.

Fact: A 100,000 word mystery from an Unknown Writer, when traditional publishing sells it, is priced EXACTLY at the same price as similar-sized novel from a bestselling writer. Price in old traditional publishing was based on printing and shipping costs and the size of the book and how many would fit in a sales and a bunch of other factors, including shipping cartons.

Fact: Not once in the last one hundred years did any traditional publisher price a new writer's book lower because the writer was unknown. (Nope, they priced it because of printing costs.)

Fact: All writers are insecure.

So in 2009 or so, here comes a workable electronic publishing that allowed writers in the door to set their own publishing businesses and thus, their own prices. And since all writers are insecure, beginning writers decided their books were worth less and thus, because they were suddenly given the control, priced their books less.

Talk about a wild and crazy time. While traditional publishers were fighting and breaking laws to not allow Amazon to lower e-book prices to $9.99 because it was *shockingly* too low, new indie writers were pricing their brand new novels at 99 cents because it couldn't be any good since they were new writers.

And thus this myth got started.

A bunch of us were fighting the trend and getting kicked for it by shouting to indie publishing writers to not cheapen their own books, just price slightly less than traditional.

And since a lot of us saw electronic books replacing mass market paperbacks, our suggestions were to price novels and collections in the same price range as mass market paperbacks. $4.99 to $7.99. Far under what New York traditional publishers thought was too low (back then and still in most cases).

But insecure writers (given price control) just won't believe that anyone will pay a decent amount of money for their book.

So the novels they spent a long time writing go into the 99 cent discount bin, the perma-free bin, or the $2.99 price.

And they always have what they think are good reasons for doing so.

Insecurity is a bitch to fight in fiction writing.

BUT NO ONE KNOWS MY NAME... (add whining here...)

Really. Go ahead, ask anyone on any street if they know my name and they will look at you puzzled. Fact: No one (but a bunch of writers who seldom buy books) knows my name either.

And they certainly didn't know all the pen names I sold books under. Every time I sold a book under a pen name, **I became a new writer. Duh.**

Only difference was, I have been learning and practicing my storytelling skills for decades, so with a new name, my books still entertained people.

Since my wife has some open pen names, I'm going to mention her name here. She writes romance under the names Kristine Grayson and Kris DeLake. She writes mystery under Kristine Kathryn Rusch, Kris Rusch, and Kris Nelscott. All her science fiction is under Kristine Kathryn Rusch. With me, she wrote five media novels under Sandy Schofield. With me, she did a bunch of movie tie-in novels under the name Kathryn Wesley. And there are others.

All of those pen names won or were nominated for awards and sold thousands and thousands of copies per book.

So she was a new writer with all those names at one point or another.

AND NOT ONE OF THOSE BOOKS WAS DISCOUNTED OR SOLD CHEAPLY BECAUSE SHE WAS A NEW WRITER WITH A NAME NO ONE RECOGNIZED. Yet, she was exactly that because no one knew her pen name.

She sold all those books and started all those brand new names because she's a great storyteller and liked to write across genres.

I had one writer become rude and downright nasty with me recently, and from what people tell me, this writer is still bad-mouthing me every chance the person gets. Why? Because I had the gall to tell this person that the reason the person had good sales was because the person was a great storyteller, not because the person had discounted books.

This person's insecurity would not allow the compliment in. Ah, well. I hit a personal button with that one I guess.

But most new writers won't be angry at me with this. They will just not believe me because, you know, I don't *understand* what they are going through. (Add sarcasm snort right here.)

As a New Writer, What Do I Do?

There are a number of things you can do, but first off, you need to understand some really basic principles of publishing.

Principle #1... Your story has to be good. I didn't say well-written, I said you have to tell a good story. This takes years to learn, but is fun to learn. And you never get to the top of the skills of storytelling. And you, as the artist, never know when you hit on a good story or missed, so you put them all out.

Principle #2... You have to have more than a few products. When a reader, through promotion or word of mouth, finds your book and reads it and likes it, they want more instantly. If you only have one or two, they will move on and forget your name. Nature of the new world.

Principle #3… A writing profession is a long-term thing. It has always been that way, but this new world has allowed writers to get in a hurry, so many get discouraged easily without a lot of sales early on. To fight this, think in chunks of five and ten years ahead, not a week or month ahead.

So understanding those principles, what can a new writer do in this modern world?

The answer is simple… TAKE CONTROL

And when I mean take control, I mean take control of EVERYTHING. And part of that will be taking control of the three principles of publishing above.

—So first, make it a focus to keep learning how to be a great storyteller. This can be learned in books, online, in workshops, and a thousand places in this modern world. But you have to develop a quick filter to ignore all the stuff that doesn't make sense to you and work for you as an artist. And make this learning a focus that will never end.

—Second, make more time to sit in the writing chair and produce product. Even an extra fifteen or thirty minutes per day will do wonders. Every writer is different and every writer has different methods to get to producing fiction that readers enjoy. At first you may not be good enough to control the quality of your stories, but you can control how many hours you spend writing original words. (Rewriting and researching are not writing.)

—Third, set up your publishing press (basics are under Think Like a Publisher under the tab above), then learn to do covers, learn to do blurbs, learn to do paper books, learn how to upload your work. Even if you end up not doing it, you need to know how to do it to take control of everything.

—Fourth, start learning copyright. And read blogs and other factors about the good and the bad of traditional publishing so you are informed if and when you are approached.

All of the above are long term and you need to plan long term. Five and ten-year chunks, remember.

For example, ask yourself this: If you are giving over cover control to someone you hire, are you going to still want to be paying that money out in five years just because you are afraid to learn how to do your own covers? Think ahead. Learning is tough, but this is an international profession. And it can be learned.

Take everything you can under your own control. Learning, production, money, everything. Give no control away because you are afraid or lazy. That way lies disaster.

The Big Things You Need to Do

These will be the hardest two things you ever have to do in this business.

#1... Believe in your own art.

#2... Be patient with sales.

To believe in your own art, you need an ego. All successful artists have egos. We protect our work and do our best with everything we do and hold pride in our work. You have to believe in yourself and your own ability to keep learning to stand any chance at all in this business.

And there will be those around you and online who have a huge desire to pull you down. Ignore them, ignore reviews, do your own work from your own heart.

And that especially means don't discount your books unless for a special sale. For example, for twenty days, people can buy one of my books right now, as I write this, for less than $1.00 electronically because it's combined in a book bundle with other novels. But on all the major sites, it's still priced as a standard novel at $6.99.

You must learn how to be patient with sales. If you use sales as a self-worth measuring stick, you are turning over to others something you can't control. And the moment you turn over to others your own self-worth, you are doomed. Write and put books and stories up for only you. The fact that some people buy them, fantastic.

And yes, if you keep doing that, at some point you will make your entire living off of what you enjoy doing. It is very possible and likely if you believe in your own art and keep producing new work and learning.

Very likely.

But it's not easy. Nothing about what I have said here is easy.

You must keep learning and keep the value on your own work. If you don't value your own work, if you don't believe in your own work, even as a new writer, no one ever will.

Every professional writer started off as a new writer. All of us took years and years to get to making a living. But the one thing we all had in common right from the start?

We all believed in our own work, protected it, and never undervalued it in any fashion.

Sacred Cow #4

YOU MUST HAVE AN AGENT TO SELL A BOOK IN TRANSLATION OVERSEAS

This myth is based out of newer writers just not knowing facts and agents trying to stay relevant in a changing world.

Some History

More than fifteen to twenty years ago, it was difficult, at best, to sell many translation rights overseas for your books that were published here in the States. It took connections and even knowing who the overseas publishers were.

Then came along this funny little invention called e-mail. And the internet.

You all know what that is, I'm sure.

And overseas publishers could get directly in contact with writers. And with the increase in writer web sites, that's how overseas publishers got hold of writers, who then in the early days, not knowing any better, (and I was no exception) just sent the overseas publisher on to my agent.

And that's just the way it was done back in those dark days where we all had to walk both ways, uphill, in the snow, just to get a book published. It was horrid, I tell you. Horrid.

But Things Have Changed

I know a lot of people, a vast number of people in agent-land and traditional publishing, don't want newer professional writers to know things have changed. They want the old system to continue. But sadly for them, and great for the rest of us, things have changed a great deal.

Some general facts:

—In general, publishing contract with any publisher outside of North America is simpler by factors and factors. And easy to read.

—In general, publishing contracts from publishers outside of North America are clear to what the translation publisher is buying.

—In general, publishing contracts from publishers outside of North America have clear termination and reversion dates in them. And often limitations on print runs without a renewal.

—In general, after the first contract or two, you can do your own and negotiating is not often done. A small fee to an intellectual property attorney will often be enough on the first one or two.

—In general, most overseas contracts, (now all translation sales) are small unless your book is really taking off. Nature of smaller markets. Modern agents often don't feel it is worth their time to do a short-term $500 contract and get $50. (Their overseas agent will take the other $50 in fee.) So they often don't bother for their clients. Far too much work for them to deal with, they feel. (I personally like a $500 sales to a translation company.)

—In general, agents HATE contracts that have limited press runs, one fee, and no royalties because that means once they have the contract done, they get no more money and have no more hold on the book. So agents will try to make an overseas contract far, far more complex and add royalties.

—In general, the biggest area for agent embezzlement is from overseas book royalties. Authors don't know they are owed money because seldom do overseas agents forward the paperwork or the money from the overseas publisher, and if they do, the money often gets stopped or "forgotten" in the states agency. Hard for an author to actually get regular overseas royalty payments.

But How Do I Sell a Book Overseas Without An Agent?

This is the area that just stunned me when I learned it about agents. About one third of all agencies in the United States farm out their overseas sales to another agency here in the States that does nothing but sell books overseas. The second agency does massive lists with hundreds and hundreds of authors' names and books on it. (Nothing more.) And they regularly ship these gigantic lists to overseas agents to try to pitch to translation companies through overseas agents.

So, the flat honest truth is that unless you are a major best-seller, your book is ignored. When you have all the writers from twenty or thirty agencies on a huge list the size of a small town phone book, trust me, only the top even get looked at. And there are no covers or blurbs. Just title and author name, and sometimes genre.

That's another ugly truth about how most agents "respect" your work and try to sell it overseas. They will flat tell you they are trying to sell your book overseas, then give the name and author name to another agency, who will add it on a list to go along with thousands of others.

So you are an indie writer. Right? How do you get your books noticed overseas?

Let me think...

Oh, yeah, **you publish the thing in all markets**. Duh.

Amazon, B&N, Kobo, iTunes, Smashwords, CreateSpace, and so on down through the smaller electronic distributors and international stores. And when you do, you click all the overseas channels.

And boom, your book is available in English worldwide.

Last month alone, Kris and I sold English language books in 26 different countries. That's so normal, we seldom notice that now, where ten years ago, that would have been a major deal.

If you have your book available worldwide in English, people all around the world will have a chance to see your book, (with cover and blurb). If editor or someone at an overseas translation house reads your book and likes it (called a submission in the old world, but today they buy it instead), and the editor thinks your book will fit their translation line, the editor will contact you directly through your own publisher web site.

Or your author web site. (You do have "contact me" tabs, don't you?)

So it goes like this so this is clear:

Step one... You publish your book through all electronic and paper outlets available. (Not just Kindle.)

Step two... Your book is available with your great cover and blurb, world-wide, for anyone to buy in English.

Step three... An editor of a translation line at a publisher in an overseas company is looking for books for his line that will fit his topic. He finds and buys your book and reads it and likes it and thinks it will fit his line of books.

Step four... The editor contacts you by e-mail.

Step five... The editor will often ask for who your representative is. You write them back and say simply. "My attorney and I handle all translation sales."

Step six... The editor will make an offer directly to you. You say you are interested depending on the terms.

Step seven... The editor e-mails you a contract, you check it for rights grabs, sign it and e-mail it back.

Step eight... The translation publisher will send you the money by Paypal, wire, or direct transfer into your bank account.

Done.

The translation publisher will send you a copy of your book in French or German or whatever when the book hits print.

It really is that simple.

Scary simple.

Since I got rid of my agent, and Kris got rid of her agent, we get many more offers from overseas publishers. The agents we had were blocking the small offers, while we take them, for the most part.

And the overseas translation publishers are finding our books because we are publishing them in English all over the world. In every format through every store. And keeping them in print all over the world.

As I said, things have changed.

So Why Is This Myth Still So Strong?

Actually, in this new world, it's logical why this myth that needing an agent to sell overseas is still strong.

1... Generally, newer professionals just feel this is scary. (It's not, if you don't panic and give it to an agent.)

2... Generally, newer professionals do not know copyright, which means they do not understand that all contracts must be done in the language of the author. (Berne Convention) They think they are going to get something in Chinese or something. Learn copyright, people.

3... Generally, agents are losing income and power by the day, so they promote this to get young, unwary professionals on board to sign their agency agreements. And many agency agreements are rights grabs of authors' works. Yet authors sign them all the time and discover the hard way they are trapped and have signed away percentages of their book for life of the copyright.

4... Generally, this area is a large money-maker for agencies because authors allow agents to have all the money and all the paperwork with that money, so overseas sales are easy to just leave in the agency accounts and misplace the paperwork. (All unintentional, of course... cough) So agents really, really push this to unwary newer professional writers and older professionals too busy to think it through.

5... Generally, authors feel that **selling** overseas in translation means they must send out stories into slush piles or something like that to get an overseas publisher to look at their work. So they think agents have the contacts, and agents pretend they do have the contacts. (Their contact is another agency here in the States.)

Authors don't realize that if they indie publish (not traditional), their books go out across the world to be seen.

And that's all there is to it.

Summary

There is no reason at all in this modern world to have an agent on an overseas translation sale. None.

—Contracts are simple and you can spend a few bucks to have an IP rights attorney look at the first two or so until you feel comfortable with what you are reading.

—Contracts are in your language and the money comes directly to you.

—Translation publishers see your book if you are publishing it in English around the world. There is no such thing as "selling" done by an agent. Your book sells itself and they find it because it's out there. (And if agent tries to convince you they can "sell your book overseas" ask them for a list of their overseas partner agencies, or ask if they go through a "specialty agency" here in the states. Either way, the agent who is telling you he will sell the book is lying, flat out. They will not. Period. They will simply hand off your book to someone else and do NO work.)

—The agent ship is going down quickly. Don't have your books trapped in their agency agreements because you are afraid of something that might take you all of thirty minutes to do.

Holding a copy of your book in translation in your hand is great fun. You might not be able to read it, but it sure feels neat.

Avoid this huge pitfall that agents are trying to sell you in desperation.

Sacred Cow #5
PRINTERS ARE DISTRIBUTORS

L et me put this in a different light to be clear.
Indie Publishers believe there are basically only two places to take their books to be printed and distributed to bookstores. CreateSpace and LightningSource.

This myth is logical because of how indie publishing came about with the ebook revolution and then slowly indie publishers (writers) started understanding that with a little extra work, they could do a paper book. But the myth that has indie writers believing they have to go to New York to get into bookstores has slowed the growth of this side of indie publishing.

Too bad.

Some Basics on Who is Who

LightningSource is owned by Ingrams (and has such a bad terms of service, no one who actually reads terms of service would go with them.)

CreateSpace is owned by Amazon.

They are both what is commonly called POD printers. In other words, they have a printing structure that will print small quantities of your book for cheap as you need them. Print On Demand.

There are a lot of other POD service printers. But CreateSpace and LightningSource get most of the press in this myth. Any Staples or Kinkos works as a POD printer as well, but prices are much higher in places like that.

You can Google and get all sorts of listings for POD printing prices and such, which vary all over the place. Wow. So caution. So far that I have found, CreateSpace is the cheapest by far for printing any perfect bound book unless you pay ahead or are up to using web presses (see below) at runs of ten thousand copies.

Some More Basics

—**Printers print your books.** Printers can be POD (copy machines), offset (high level color), or web press (newspaper and pulp paper). Publisher's choice.

—**Distributors distribute your book.** A distributor can distribute your book in limited ways, or into the big trade publishing channels. That will depend totally on how you want your book distributed. As a publisher, you have control of that.

Printers charge by a per page or per copy price.

Distributors usually take a cut of any books sold. Often to get good placement, the publisher pays a distributor some fees as well. All depends on the contract the publisher (you) negotiated with the distributor. The more books you want them to distribute, the better your deal.

The Problem With This Myth

Printers such as CreateSpace, LightningSource, and others, such as Lulu, have a part of their business where they will distribute the book into the trade channels. For writers who don't understand there is a difference between a printer and a distributor, this seems like a logical connection.

In fact, most POD printers I saw will sell your book on their own web site and into basic channels such as Ingrams and Baker and Taylor, two of the major distributors.

And honestly, the distribution services offered by CreateSpace have been wonderful for the indie publishers to get paper books out into bookstores. (See early myth on this topic as to how easy that has become.)

But just lately, WMG Publishing was planning on doing some hardbacks on a few special projects. So we were going to go easy and go with LightningSource until we read the terms of service and decided we didn't want to give them copyrights to our books. So I shrugged and said that when we are ready, we'll just use a binder in Portland, Oregon, or maybe one near Seattle. There are, to my knowledge, without really looking that hard, almost ten quality binders in the Portland/Seattle area.

And I found two that were cheaper than LightningSource.

So it would work this way. We would have CreateSpace print the books, ship them directly to the bindery, and have a local hardback bindery bind the books into hard cases.

So besides selling them ourselves off our own web site or putting them on Amazon (which you can do), if we wanted to get these hardbacks we had bound locally into national distribution, what would we do?

Simple: We would go to a distributor and set up a deal to work with them to get the book into the trade book channels.

KILLING THE TOP TEN SACRED COWS OF INDIE PUBLISHING

(Meaning into the major distributors and to the major stores such as B&N and other stores.) And for those of you wondering, hardbacks are full copy returnable, and many distributors have no-returns programs you can get into.

(I can now hear the question... But where would we find a distributor? I didn't even know they existed.)

For a start, **and only a start**, the *Independent Book Publishers Association* has a pretty good list of book distributors. (Bet most of you indie publishers out there didn't even know the IBPA even existed, did you? (grin)) Now EXTREME caution with this organization and joining it because, to be honest, they haven't moved into this century yet. If they do, it might be something worthwhile to join. So caution, eyes open, I am not recommending them at this point.

But they do have a good list of distributors. Go look at that at least. http://www.ibpa-online.org/resources/distributor-wholesalers/

Now I need to be very, very clear here. If you are not acting in your business completely like a publisher, this won't work. And if you do not have a pretty good list of books and have a schedule ahead of upcoming books, chances are most of these distributors will not work with you. They might work with someone who calls themselves a self-published author, but it would be tougher. (But I expect everyone reading this to be acting like a publisher, have a publishing imprint on their books, and a growing book list.)

Why Printer as Distributor Myth Damages Writers and Indie Publishers

Simple, really. This belief system that CreateSpace or LighteningSource or Lulu are the only way to print or distribute often forces writers and indie publishers into bad decisions. Granted, at the moment, it is a cheap and easy way to print and get into the system. But there are drawbacks to this cheap and easy system.

Running through an established distributor and into the trade system will get your books into better discount ranges to bookstores. You can get out of some of the lower level book catalogs on Ingrams and B&T. And often a good distributor will help in marketing and getting the word to their bookstore customers that they have a new book from you.

That might be worth it to some of you out there.

To work with these distribution people, you have to be doing a lot of things correctly, including pricing. And acting as a publisher as I said.

I understand that most reading this, including WMG Publishing, will be content to ride the horse we are on at the moment, which is CreateSpace.

But we know the options, we know that if something suddenly happened to CreateSpace, we would just continue right on publishing paper books and getting our books into stores.

Summary

Printers are very, very different from distributors. You have different printers in your own local town that can print books. Maybe not cheaply, but they can do it.

Distributors are companies that can get your printed books into the trade system (exactly the same as traditional publishers) and get your books to the same places.

CreateSpace and the other POD printers have a distribution arm. But here at WMG Publishing we often click off all distribution and just buy our books direct from CreateSpace. **They are**

just a printer at that point. For example, we do that when we are doing a large order of ARCs.

Printers are not distributors. Some printers have a distribution side, but you do not have to use it.

So keep your mind open and the two forms of business apart in thinking and you, as an indie publisher, will make better decisions.

Sacred Cow #6

I CAN PUT A BOOK UP FOR SALE
AND LEAVE IT FOREVER

or conversely...

IF I PUT A BOOK UP FOR SALE,
I HAVE TO CHANGE IT EVERY WEEK

This double-headed myth is a real killer to income and books. A paraphrased conversation I had with a friend sort of sums up this myth.

A friend of mine said, "Joe Konrath says that as indie writers, we must tend our gardens."

I agreed, but added, "And we need to learn when to leave the garden alone to grow as well."

I have heard both sides of this myth a lot, and I'm sure early on in this new indie world, I advocated one side or the other a few times myself, more than likely far more than a few times.

Now I advocate walking a line on balance.

Some History

For a century and more, books had no staying power, for the most part. There were always books that survived in the used and rare world. Sure. But rarely did a book outside that world survive in any fashion, with a few exceptions.

The exceptions were the very, very unusual books that found new readers generation after generation and that publishers kept the books in print.

In modern publishing, those books tended to be classics, or young adult books. In fact, for a few decades, the backlist (older books) in young adult sold better than the front list (new books put out that year).

Sadly, very, very few genre books were kept in print for very long. Even classics and major award winners are lost and out of print, unless brought back into print by a small press.

But the publishers of those books that had a long life were doing what indie writers need to learn to do. Every four or five years, they would put on an updated new cover, or reissue the book with some sort of fanfare, or some other new promotion. (Note: I said every few years, not every other month.)

But for the majority of all books published in the last century, the print runs were either limited, or the book was considered disposable.

The disposable aspect of books came from two major places. First came World War Two, where paperbacks were included as supplies to the soldiers to be read and passed around and then tossed away. Second, publishers started to just ask for covers back of many books in the returns system to save on shipping, so the bookstores would strip the covers and get credit for the unsold books.

After decades, books to traditional publishers became like bananas on a fruit stand. If they didn't sell quickly, they spoiled and thus were destroyed, put out of print, and forgotten.

Books became produce. (And sadly, to traditional publishers, they still are. Plus they have become assets of a corporate balance sheet even if they are out of print or only for sale in a bad and expensive electronic edition.)

Up until the last five years or so, and the rise of the electronic book, this was the feelings for books *and how authors felt about them as well.*

I can't believe how many times I heard from authors in traditional publishing that you were only as good as your last book. (I'm sure I said that myself a few times along the way, and I believed it because I worked in traditional publishing.)

So this idea that indie writers now have books they can publish and keep in print for a long time is great. But they publish it and then what do they do? And here comes this dual-sided myth.

Indie writers tend to fall into two crazy camps.

Camp One: They put the book up and change the price weekly and the cover monthly.

Camp Two: They put the book up and forget it.

There is a balance point in the center of the two camps, which is where the analogy of tending a garden comes in perfectly.

Indie writers, in this case, must learn from how traditional publishers treated classics and bestselling young adult books. The traditional publishers kept those books alive and selling for decades.

Indie writers can do the same thing if they know what they are doing.

The Silliness of Both Sides

To start off, you must learn to look at books with a long view into the future. Very few writers do this.

Very, very few.

Almost no writer I know looks at books as an investment that could pay off over decades.

So let me use the "tend the garden" analogy to show the two extremes.

The Care-Too-Much problem.

You plant some corn seeds in your garden. (That's publishing your book to be clear.)

Come back the next day, nothing is happening to the seeds in your garden, so you give them more water, sit in the window watching, nothing happens, water it more, watch more.

Nothing.

On day three, since there is nothing happening yet, you decide you must have planted the seeds in the wrong place, so you dig up the seeds and move them, give them more water, plant them again.

Sit and watch for something to happen. Maybe you put the seeds too deep, so you dig them up again and bring them right to the surface.

Watch. Two days later nothing.

You panic.

So you dig the seeds up again and bury them deeper because you read on a blog somewhere that's what you should do.

And on and on and on.

You get the picture I hope. Books are like corn. They are not magic, they take time to find an audience. Books take time to grow an audience.

So what about the other side of this? The Put The Book Up and Forget Problem.

You decide to plant corn in your garden. You plant the seeds. (Again this is publishing a book.)

You walk away from your garden and go back to work and don't even bother to water anything or weed anything. In six months or a year or two you look at it again and the corn is dead, buried under weeds.

Note that neither extreme works well.

Most indie writers I have met are the first example, not giving anything time to grow or live, messing with it all the time.

I tend to fall in the second camp far too much because of my training that books are written and then gone. So I plant seeds and forget them and do nothing to help anything along.

Both sides of this myth do not produce good LONG TERM product year after year.

A Way Out of the Two-Sided Myth

Perspective is the way to the center from both sides of this myth.

And continuing to learn about how book buyers find books helps as well.

So using Kris and myself as an example here, and what I did when electronic books got started, let me show you some aspects of both sides, and the problems of both sides.

Way back when Kindle first opened the KDP program, a friend taught a number of other writers and me how to get books onto Kindle and Smashwords. (I have detailed in other places how I slowly came to realize how my backlist, with this new system, was a gold mine waiting to be tapped.)

So as with most things I do, I jumped in and went to work. My attitude back then was I needed to get as many titles up as I could as fast as I could.

It was just me doing all the work, and I was putting up my own stories and Kris's short stories and then eventually we started putting up some backlist novels.

And one and a half years later, I had over 200 titles up on Kindle, Smashwords, and B&N.

I had not gone back and looked at a one of them. Just put the book or story up and moved to the next one.

After a year and a half, the books were making enough money that we could hire some fulltime help. Since we had started a major publishing company once before (Pulphouse Publishing in 1987), we knew where this was heading, so we created a corporation and found the best person to run the business.

All paid for because I had pushed over 200 plus titles up and left them alone.

Allyson Longueira came on board and after looking at everything for a month and getting herself up to speed, she came to me and Kris and said simply, "We need to change everything, every cover, everything we have up so far. And we need to re-proof everything and redo all the blurbs."

In other words, I had paid no attention to the garden and it was covered in weeds and the income was about to be choked off if we didn't do some weeding and new planting and repairing.

You see, my covers sucked. I had done them in Powerpoint quickly. And the blurbs I hadn't paid the slightest bit of attention to, and proofing was lax on those early books. We often used the traditional publisher printed versions of our stories and those, as are most traditional published books, were riddled with mistakes.

Allyson was right. At the two-year mark after I started putting stuff up as fast as I could, we needed to tend that garden.

Desperately.

She started fixing things, and we put up some new books as well, and we started working on the old blurbs and took off the worst offending covers fairly quickly. By the time she had been with us for six months, our title count was up to 250 titles, and she wasn't a quarter of the way through fixing the old stuff.

But the garden was starting to look better at least.

And the income was increasing, especially since the new work we put up was much better in look, blurbs, and proofing.

And readers of indie books were starting to expect better at this point in indie publishing and we were shifting to give it to them.

The extra money coming in allowed us to hire more help in WMG Publishing. About a year after hiring Allyson, we had enough to start the audio department as well.

After one year, we had managed to fix all but a few of those early titles I had done quickly, and our title count was over 300 titles.

That's a very large garden, let me tell you.

Now, another year plus has past, we are over 400 titles and climbing, and almost all but a very few have been touched and fixed from those early days. And many of the first changes Allyson did when she started have also been changed out again.

We have branded the covers and books on the major series and are in the process of branding to series and to genre the minor series as well.

We have a proofreader on staff, a full-time promotions person coming on board in a month, and a second and third sales team members coming on board this fall.

Now understand, when I say the word "we" in that above story, it's not me anymore doing much besides writing checks. Sure, I do *Smith's Monthly* covers and layout and I help edit *Fiction River* and that's it.

In fact, right now I spend most of my daylight time working on online workshops, which I love and keep me learning.

Kris and I do not run WMG Publishing and haven't now for more than a year. Allyson is the publisher, we call her the boss, and she runs the business and the seven or eight employees and works with the authors in *Fiction River* and so on.

Kris and I created an indie/traditional publisher hybrid.

Honestly, many bestselling authors who are leaving publishing are doing the same sorts of things in various forms, hiring help for many aspects that are needed in this new indie world.

Kris and I let the money coming from the indie publishing build the business. We plowed every cent back into the growth. And we still are.

In other words, we are investing our income in our future.

So now our garden is well-tended, unlike what it was back three years ago. It is expanding every month as Kris and I continue to add in new backlist and keep writing new front list books and stories as well. I would imagine our title count will be past five hundred by the end of 2014.

And *Fiction River* has brought in many other authors and editors and WMG has plans to expand into many new projects as time and money allow.

How did we do this? Honestly, we found a balance between leaving the garden alone and spending too much time on every title.

At four hundred plus titles, we can't pay attention to every title, and yes, some get forgotten for a time, so we still lean a little too much to the put-up-and-forget side of things. But that will be changing a lot as 2014 goes on.

Suggestions to Find a Balance

The WIBBOW test was coined by professional writer Scott William Carter. WIBBOW stands for:

Would I Be Better Off Writing?

For indie writers, the answer is almost always yes. As I discovered as I pounded up over 200 different backlist titles from Kris and my decades of writing, new product sells old product.

The best promotion is always the next book.

But covers must be tended to and as your knowledge grows about covers, you must fix covers every three or four year. Sometimes genre trends just move in looks. You need to stay abreast of the changes. (That takes research time as well.)

As you get better at writing sales copy instead of plot summaries, your blurbs need to be fixed.

To get the book in the right place, you also need to keep learning genre. That's critical to sales.

And then there is that ugly topic of pricing, which I will talk about in the 9th Sacred Cows of Indie Publishing coming up shortly.

So here are my suggestions to find a balance, since I have been in this since the beginning of this crazy movement, and also spent decades in traditional publishing.

Publish the book with the best modern-looking cover to genre you can do, with the best blurb, and with luck in the right spot in the bookstores.

Get the book into as many places as you can, from Kindle to Kobo to B&N to iBooks to Smashwords to audio to paper editions. Everywhere. You must try to find as many readers as you can.

Tell your social media, your friends, your family, get it to a few bloggers, and other minor promotions you may do, and that's it. WIBBOW test.

Go back to writing. Write the next book. DO NOT TOUCH THE PREVIOUS BOOK.

Check your sales every month at the end of the month. Not sales numbers, but **income** from that book. Let me say that again. **Track INCOME.** You need to track what each book (title) is making you per month total from all the sites. (TrackerBox program can do this for you.)

After one year, look at the sales figures for each of your titles. If one title is not selling hardly at all, time to take a look at it. Check first the location on the shelf, the genre. Have a friend read it and see if your idea of the genre matches your friend's. If it does, then look at the blurb. If it is full of plot and passive verbs, learn how to rewrite that into sales language. Then have someone look at your cover and tell you the truth about it. Somehow who knows commercial book covers.

Fix what needs to be fixed on all under performing titles, and go back to writing. In other words, tend the garden and let things continue to grow.

With every title, novel, short story, or collection, check the sales after one year to see if they are on track.

In the next chapter of Killing the Top Ten Sacred Cows of Indie Publishing, I talk about the myth of small sales numbers. So that will help you understand how to judge when a book is selling well and when it is under performing and needs tending.

Summary

This myth can really kill sales and entire writer's careers.

On one side, the example of waiting for growth every few days in a garden, the myth can cause extreme disappointment. And frustration. And it can kill writing of new projects and titles.

The other side of putting up and ignoring doesn't allow your books to change with the times, doesn't allow you to follow under-performing titles, and flat isn't good business when you have a valuable property.

Each title is a property. Remember that. Putting the title up and ignoring it for too long would be like building a house and then just letting it sit, not doing anything to it to keep it up. It might be fine for a time, but eventually it will need work and repair.

So find a balance between too much change on a title and too little change.

But my biggest suggestion to everyone is think of publishing as a long-term business.

Think in units of years, not units of days.

Give readers time to find your work, to read your work, to enjoy your work.

Tend your garden. But don't overwater it on one side, or let the weeds and lack of care choke it out on the other.

Find a balance.

And have fun.

Sacred Cow #7

I HAVE TO SELL A LOT OF COPIES VERY QUICKLY OR MY BOOK IS A FAILURE

Of course, this shows no understanding of property and long-term return on investment. But most writers wouldn't know that, so they get trapped in this thinking all the time.

And when **expectations of sales** do not match actual sales, writers often quit writing, or make really silly decisions like lowering prices for no good business or promotion reason. When decisions are made out of panic that a book isn't selling up to some made-up expectation, then nothing but problems arise.

Some History

Interestingly enough, this myth is based solidly out of the way traditional publishers think. And for a bunch of indie writers who pride themselves in thinking and acting differently, following traditional publishing thinking in this makes me shake my head in wonder.

First:

For the last thirty or so years, traditional publishers tracked the success or failure quickly of a book, not on how many sold at first, but on books shipped. And if a book didn't ship up to expectations (meaning orders placed ahead of the book's ship date didn't match a made-up number on a profit-and-loss sheet), then the book was deemed a failure and quickly dropped out of print.

And the author would have an awful time selling more books under that author name.

Second:

Bestseller lists for traditional publishers relied on a combination of books shipped and books sold in certain stores in a week-long period. So if that book didn't sell quickly and in large numbers, the book didn't make a bestseller list.

Third:

With very few exceptions, traditional publishers for thirty or more years considered books to be like produce at a grocery store. There was limited shelf space, so if a book didn't sell, it was destroyed and the covers returned for credit, or if it was a hardback, the entire book was shipped back to the publisher for credit.

For the longest time, returns under 50% were considered good sales and returns over 50% in a short period of time, the book was a failure.

So here comes indie publishing, with the ability to think long term, unlike traditional publishers. Indie publishers can plan sales on a book for a ten-year or twenty-year plan.

Traditional publishers flat can't do that with the quarterly demand of profits for their corporate masters. They must churn the profit, kill books that don't sell quickly, and move on to the next book.

This chapter I hope will give a few indie publishers a different perspective on sales. But that myth that has come from traditional publishers (that books must sell a lot and very quickly) is a very, very deep and hard myth to crack for most.

Some Math

First Traditional Publishing

In this world at the moment, if you sold a genre book to a traditional publisher and got a $4,000 advance, you would be expected to sell about 3,000 copies in six months total before it vanished and dropped into the weed-filled garden (see last post) of electronic book sales just dripping along.

3,000 initial sales. That's after returns and I assume you are smart enough if you are reading this to not have an agent taking a piece of that $4,000.

Let's make one more assumption: None of your sales are to high discount stores.

So you would get 6% of the $7.99 cover price per sale for the mass market paper. Or about 48 cents per sale for paper.

For electronic sales you would get 25% of net. Publisher puts it up at $7.99 electronic. That's about $1.40 per sale ($7.99 x 70% x 25%).

Half of the 3,000 copies to be successful for this book are electronic sales, half are paper sales.

Paper: 1,500 sales x $.48 = $720

Electronic 1,500 sales x $1.40 = $2,100

Your book earned out $2,820 of the $4,000 advance.

The $4,000 is all the money you will ever see on that genre book.

Let me be generous and say it took only three years from the moment you wrote the book to the book became a wilted piece of produce to the publisher. (Chances are it took closer to four years, but let's go with three.)

And remember, you won't get that book back. It will continue to trickle sales in electronic form (because the publisher won't care anymore, the book is just out there, so the garden for that book is not being tended). And at 25% of net, you might as well just forget that book until you can get the copyright reverted at 35 years.

Indie Publisher Math

I'm going to make some major assumptions here. I am going to assume that you have a paper edition of your book and you have your book available in all the different major online bookstores direct so you are getting paid monthly.

So in electronic editions, you price your novel at $6.99. (Below what your traditional publisher would have priced it.) So you will be making approximately $4.90 per sale

In paper you price your book so that in the extended distribution you get at least $2.00 per sale.

You put your book up in all electronic venues (Kindle, B&N, iBooks, Kobo, GooglePlay, Smashwords, and so on) your book sells 20 copies the first month total across all sites.

And 5 copies in paper the first month.

So in one month your income is $108.00. ($98.00 electronic plus $10 paper.) And you are thinking your book is a failure after the first month.

I am going to be making another assumption. I am going to assume that as time goes on, every year or two, you tend your garden. (See Chapter Six.)

So over the next few months, your book sales grow slightly, but then they come down some toward the end of the first year, so that you are averaging over the entire first year of the book being in print the 25 sales per month.

So in that first year you made ($108.00 x 12) $1,296.00

In the same three years at that rate, without you doing much but some minor tending of the garden, you will have made $3,888.00.

Almost exactly in the same amount of time, the same amount of money you would have made in traditional publishing.

Only difference is that you still have the book and it's still earning for you into the future, where with traditional you don't own it anymore and won't for a very long time.

25 copies sales per month.

At that level, it's a book that many indie publishers would think is a complete failure.

I won't even go into the million things you could do to help the sales of that book, such as writing more books, writing more books in the same world, learning how to do better covers and switch the cover out in a couple of years, and so on.

Yeah, a success selling it to traditional publishing for $4,000 dollars, but a failure at 25 copies sales per month?

And that's this myth.

Look at the Difference in Sales Numbers

The traditional publisher managed to shove out 3,000 copies of the book, half electronic, half paper, and still didn't come close to earning you back your $4,000 advance.

You ended up with almost the same amount of money by selling 720 electronic copies total in three years and 180 copies in paper in three years.

But you will, even at that pace, eventually sell the 1,500 copies of the electronic books in just over six years and the full 1,500 copies of the paper in around twenty or so years assuming your paper sales do not increase over time.

And when you end up with that amount of sales on the book, you will have made on that book ($4.90 x 1,500) $7,350 electronic and $3,000 paper.

Over $10,000 total and you will still own and can be selling the book into the future.

So Why Do Indie Publishers Hold Onto this Myth?

Basically, we all want our books to sell well, have a lot of fans, and hope that it gets read everywhere. That's just common sense.

But the problem arises when a book doesn't sell as well as "expected" and the indie publisher starts making bad decisions about the book.

So what is "expected?"

I like the average of 25 sales per month over all platforms. I like that expectation, and it allows me to have great fun when something jumps with more sales. And after a year or so, if book isn't selling to that "expected" average, it's time to tend the garden.

That's my expectation. But I know a ton of indie writers who would think that expectation far, far too low.

The statement those indie writers say to me is this: "I want to make a living with my writing within five years. I can't do that with sales like that."

Sadly, I just laugh when someone says that to me, and I really shouldn't. As I said before, this is a tough myth to crack.

Making a Living... More Math

Start with the amount needed to make a living. Let's just use a nice round number like $40,000 gross income. Low, but not too low. You pick your own number.

You know that every novel you are going to put up will have an average income of about $1,296 per year selling 25 copies total per month across all platforms, including paper. (Average means some books will sell more, some less, but average over all your titles.)

So take $40,000.00 and divide by $1,296.00 and you get the number 30. Thirty novels to be making $40,000 per year in five years.

5 years into 30 novels means you need to write 6 novels per year. One every-other-month.

I CAN'T DO THAT! (I hear the screams...)

Wow, that's sad you are stuck in that myth as well. Don't you folks watch my Writing in Public blog every day?

So to the math...

250 words is one manuscript page for this discussion.

A novel is 80,000 words long for this discussion.

80,000 words divided by 250 words is 320 pages for the novel.

You have 60 days in two months. So to do around 320 pages in two months, you must average around 5 pages per day.

Most writers I know do about 4 pages in an hour, so that means you need to spend generously 1.5 hours per day writing to be making a living with your writing in five years.

And then, if you kept writing, the amount of money you make would just keep going up every year.

So your books sell horribly by your expected standards. You only sell 25 copies in a month of your most recent novel.

Write six books a year and you'll be making a nice living even with your books selling horribly.

Unless, of course, you let the thinking from traditional publishing into the picture and start making bad decisions or get depressed and stop writing. Then you won't make a living in writing in five years. You'll just be bitter and sad and will have lost a dream, all because you let this myth get into your head.

Sadly, I've watched that with a bunch of indie writers around me already.

Quick Side Note on Investing

For those of you who understand investing, I did an entire lecture in the lecture series on thinking of writing as an investment.

Using this math, let me show you quickly how that works and if you want more about this way of thinking, take that lecture.

First question is: What is my investment in the book?

Some round numbers… 100 hours of writing. 10 hours of production. 10 hours of misc promotion. 120 hours of time per novel. Figure your time is worth $20.00 per hour to you have $2,400 in time.

Set costs… Copyediting (proofing) about $400. Art and misc costs $200 to make this simple.

Total costs are $3,000 per book (counting your time at $20 per hour.)

Most investors are happy with a 10% return on investment per year.

Your book is a $3,000 investment. To make a 10% investment return on your book, you need to sell $300 per year. Far, far under that $1,296.00 sales number at 25 copies.

In fact, selling six copies total per month would get you a 10% return on your investment.

Just another way to try to get some perspective on this myth that your book needs to sell a lot of copies quickly.

Sure, we all want that. But those of us with some perspective can do just fine with sales just chugging right along slowly.

Publishing as a Long Game

When I got serious about my writing finally and found Heinlein's Rules in 1982 and really started writing and learning, I hoped to be making a living with my writing in ten years.

And I purposely kept my expenses on the bottom. I drove an old used car and worked only as much as I needed to work my day jobs so that I had more time to write. As it turned out, it took me about five years, but even then I was adding to my early writing income with editing and publishing gigs.

I was lucky to make it in five years and I knew it. I'm not counting the seven years before that where I was lost in the rewriting myths. But if you count from my first sale, it's twelve years.

Indie writers who are in a hurry make bad decisions. Publishing on both sides of this fence is a long game.

Summary:
Suggestions to Help With this Myth

1... Always be focused on writing the next book.

2... Do what you can to promote when you release a book, but watch your time. Writing the next book is far more important in the long run.

3... Have a five or ten year plan and then work your writing schedule into it. If you really can't spend an hour a day at your writing, (barring major life events) than maybe you should not be thinking about making a living. Nothing at all wrong with writing being your love, not your living.

4… Keep learning how to become a better storyteller. Writing more entertaining books tends to bring more sales.

5… Do all the standard stuff to help your sales, such as having a publisher name and a publisher web site as well as an author web site. Do a newsletter and some social media, but again watch your time.

6… Only look at your numbers every month and no more often. Then don't worry about book sales numbers, just write down how much each title (book) has earned you each month.

7… Do not change anything about a book, the cover, the blurbs, nothing. Only allow yourself to change something at the year anniversary of the book being published. And if it is selling at the base level you hope to have, leave the book alone and look at it in another year.

8… Make sure you are staying abreast of all changes and keep your books in as many markets as you can directly.

9… When life knocks you down, which it will do almost every year, climb back on and just keep going. Five year or ten year plan will have many failures and missed months along the way. Adjust as you go and don't quit.

10… Focus on writing the next book.

The key with this myth is to ignore what is coming at you from other writers about speed of sales. And move away from traditional publishing produce thinking that if your book doesn't sell quickly it will spoil.

Make your five-year business plan and set your expectations.

If you have only one book up, selling 25 copies per month is unrealistic. Don't expect it. *And hoping to be lucky is not a business plan.*

But if you have a bunch of novels out and you are in the second year, selling 25 copies average across your titles is realistic. It might not happen, but it is worth aiming for.

Plus, if you also write short stories, they can help. Collections sell pretty well. Not as well as novels, but they can help in the total income.

Stop looking at sales numbers and hoping for huge sales numbers.

Plan for five or ten years out and focus on writing the next book. And have fun.

Sacred Cow #8
I HAVE MISSED MY CHANCE

…or in similar think…

I AM SO FAR BEHIND, WHY BOTHER STARTING?

This myth, of course, has a lot of origins, but the biggest one is the totally false thinking that this indie world is a gold rush. Nope. It's not anymore. Indie publishing is now a new part of publishing here to stay for any foreseeable future.

And it might, if some people are correct, become the dominant form of publishing. Who knows.

Some History

Most people think that indie publishing has only been around now since Amazon one fine day opened its doors in the KDP program. (snort)

Sorry, I have a really hard time even keeping a straight face with that kind of statement. It shows a complete lack of understanding of the publishing business.

Fact: Indie publishing (formally called small press publishing) has been around in publishing since the beginning of publishing in this modern world, which means clear back to the start of the United States and even before.

Kris and I started an indie (small press) publisher in 1987 called Pulphouse Publishing. And we did POD printing for our books, worked with a small bindery, and sold to bookstores just like the big traditional publishers did.

So indie publishing has been around a very, very long time.

Edger Rice Burroughs started an indie press in 1923 to publish his own books. (It is still in existence, by the way. Called Edger Rice Burroughs Inc. Now that's some future planning.)

But this new world that has made it very, very possible for writers with no knowledge of the publishing business to get their books to readers directly. That ability for nonprofessional writers has only been around since the KDP program started up.

Those early few years of this new wave happened fast, first with the KDP program, followed by Smashwords, and then B&N opening up their bookstores. That was followed by the POD programs to get paper into regular bookstores. All those changes happened seemingly instantly and every indie publisher seemed to be in a huge hurry.

We were no exception to that in those first few years. It felt like a gold rush, no doubt.

But then everything settled. The explosive growth of electronic books has slowed to a tiny and healthy growth. We are now in a new normal.

Granted, there are major changes coming in publishing because of disruptive technology hitting big companies not capable of handling the changes. But for indie publishers, we are now playing on a level field with all traditional publishers.

But I'm Behind!

My questions to you, if you are feeling that you are behind are this?

"Who are you behind and when did it become a race?"

I know Kris and I are sure not racing anyone. We have our business plan, we are staying out of all debt, and putting up new tittles as we can. Our pace, WMG Publishing Inc. pace, is just our pace. We are not in a race with anyone.

And to be honest, other than to learn from other indie publishers, we don't care what others do. If someone does something that makes sense for us and seems to work, we might try it when the time is right.

We don't try to chase any fad or stay even with anyone.

We just do what we do.

The problem with this myth about being behind is that it causes writers to just not start.

It's easier to just sit and feel sorry for yourself that you missed some imaginary boat than to actually make a business plan and start.

On the door of my office I have a sign that is a quote that I have no idea who said it and don't really care to look it up.

I see it every single time I walk into my writing office. There is a reason it is on my office door.

The sign says, *"...there are two kinds of people in this world, those who wish and those who will, and the world and its goods will always belong to those who will."*

How to Get Out of the Feeling of Being Behind

— First off, stop comparing yourself to other people.

Look around at what other indie publishers are doing and learn and adopt ideas that work for you and ignore all the rest.

— Ask yourself a simple question. "Do I want to be in this exact spot five years from now?"

If the answer is no, then start figuring out where you want to be in five years and in ten years. For those of you without any sense of business, this is called "Making a Business Plan."

— Be realistic in your planning. Do not set up failure, set up success.

For example, if you have never written three novels in one year, then don't have a business plan that has you creating three novels a year for five years. Remember, you can always change your business plan later when you actually produce three novels in a year.

Some people use my daily blogs as motivation. But don't try to match me from a dead stop. I have produced ten short novels in ten months while doing this blog. And about thirty short stories and parts of a bunch of other stuff on the fiction side, plus four nonfiction books. But I knew I could write a dozen short novels in a year, year after year, (my plan with my *Smith's Monthly* magazine) because I wrote eleven 90,000 word novels in one year once. And ten another year. I knew what it would take and I set my business plan for that.

— Figure in time to learn, to keep getting knowledge.

If you assume you will just "get better" in five years without study, wow are you delusional. Doesn't work that way in any art or any business.

Learning must be part of your business plan in both business and writing skills, even if you get most of that from talking with other writers and reading blogs and buying a few books. Do something to focus on learning.

— **Set a start date.**

That is the most critical advice I can give you. After you have made a plan, set a start day to get going and then just get going.

— **And keep going when life is nasty to you.**

This is the real difference between short-term careers in writing and long-term careers. All of us old-timers who have been around for three or four or more decades have had life kick us to the ground a number of times. No writer gets through a decade without huge problems that stop everything cold.

When you get back on your feet and look around, you might feel behind. That's natural. Clear that, pick a start date, take a deep breath, and start again.

Summary

The feeling of being behind, of missing a chance, hits all of us.

I am no exception. I had been going strong when my friend died three years ago and I lost a year to dealing with that estate. I somehow managed to stand up again, clear the feeling about the lost time, and reset a new business plan.

Those of you who have watched me writing in public the last ten months saw clearly that I had a few really bad months in the winter. I just kept plowing on through.

That's how this works.

"...there are two kinds of people in this world, those who wish and those who will, and the world and its goods will always belong to those who will."

So push aside the feeling of being behind, of feeling like you have missed out, set a business plan, and become a person who will...

Trust me, writing and publishing and having readers buy your books is a ton more fun than sitting around wishing.

And you all know how I like to have fun with my writing.

Sacred Cow #9
YOU MUST SELL YOUR BOOKS CHEAPLY TO MAKE ANY MONEY

This myth is so nasty, it causes huge fights among indie writers. And the reason is that every indie writer believes they are right in their way of doing things in pricing. And yet wrong pricing, either too cheap or too expensive, can really hurt sales.

So what is the right answer? What is the right price?

That depends.

Some History

Back when electronic books came in, and when KDP opened up the gates to allow indie small press publishers in the door, electronic books were still a very new thing. Electronic books composed somewhere around a half of 1% of all books sold, if that.

But when those gates opened, authors, for the very first time had the complete freedom to value their own work to readers. And with that freedom came some very interesting decisions.

Authors had to balance value with discounts to get readers to buy in a new delivery form for fiction.

First off, a bunch of traditional published writers, me included, had a sense that electronic books had less value (we were used to paper so we could be forgiven that thinking early on). So when we started into selling electronic books, we priced our books at the lowest point allowed, which was 99 cents.

Joe Konrath, a traditionally published writer was the leader of this 99-cent movement.

But as time wore on in that first early stage, and it looked like ebooks were here to stay and were growing, many of us started realizing that we could price our books higher, but still lower than traditional publishers and make a ton of money and still give readers good deals. We didn't need to toss our books into the discount bin of 99 cents just to make a few sales.

In other words, readers were starting to value electronic books.

Traditional publishers helped indie publishers a lot in this very early period by deciding that they didn't like electronic books and priced them up near hardcover levels, as if an ebook was a specialty item.

And for a time, they postponed ebook releases for a year after the hardback as they used to do with mass market paperbacks.

After a year or so, I looked at both sides with head-shaking puzzlement. No way in hell was I going to get 35 cents for a sale of a novel (My share if I published a novel for 99 cents). I got a lot more per book in royalties than that from New York on a paperback sale.

But on the flip side, there was no way in hell was I going to price a novel in electronic form at $15.99.

Publishing needed a middle ground.

At this point, the traditional publishers got together to break the law and hold prices high and stop discounting. And indie publishers were still fighting among themselves about the right low price, racing to the bottom as I liked to call it.

After another year or so, what started to become clear as electronic books exploded in sales was that readers were buying electronic books in place of mass market paperbacks, the pocket-sized books that sold around $7.99. In fact, over the last few years, the mass market form of book continues to shrink in sales almost in direct relation to the growth in ebooks sales.

So it seemed to a lot of us that a logical place to price a novel was in the area just under the price of a mass market paperback. (The $4.99 to $7.99 price range.) That allowed authors to get the most value for their work and allowed readers to get a deal.

Eventually, the strident discount sellers in the indie world, including Joe Konrath, slowly brought their prices up. And the people running traditional publishing slowly brought some of their prices down into the $7.99 to $9.99 range for an electronic book.

So now, as I write this here in the middle of 2014, pricing on electronic books, in most cases, has stabilized in a range for novels.

That price range tends to be $2.99 to $9.99 for genre fiction novels, with the indie writers being on the $2.99 side (some at 99 cents still) and the traditional publishers being on the $9.99 side of the scale (some at $15.99 still).

The Danger of the Myth

To this day, you hear the indie writers shouting about pricing in the low ranges, saying everyone needs to do that. And that low range from 99 cents to $2.99 for a full novel has become known as a discount range.

But so many indie writers don't have a clue what the word "discount" even means.

And to make matters worse, new writers think, because they don't know business, they think their new novel has no value. What they don't realize is if they had sold their novel to a traditional publisher, it would have sold fine at the high price range.

So the beginning writers price their novel at the bottom of the scale out of sheer fear and being in a hurry to make as much as possible.

For them, that first bloom of sales often quickly vanishes, or in this new world of readers becoming aware, the sales don't happen much at all. And the new writer feels hopeless, stops writing, follows the myths of promotion, and lowers their price even more.

And eventually the new writer can see no reason to write the next book because they made so little money. Deadly.

Because of pricing and getting in a hurry, their dream is shattered.

What is Discounting?

I'm going to make this scary simple. Those of you who really understand publishing, don't laugh. I'm trying to make this plain and clear.

Discounting in the book industry comes in two forms.

The first form is the chains of stores called "discount stores" that take remainders from publishers, or buy cheap books published directly into the discount sales channels. (Book Warehouse is only one of a number of such bookstore chains. You usually find them in discount malls.)

The sale books you see up front in a B&N store are discount books, published for those shelves only, or high-discount books sold by the publisher for that table. (Authors make little or no money on high discount books sold like that.)

In this same area, there are the discount bins and tables that most indie bookstores have. Those are filled with books that didn't sell that the bookstore owner just wants out of the way. One indie owner here in our town has a cart that wheels out onto the front area of the store and it's full of ten-cent books.

The second form of discount is what are simply called sales. Amazon or GooglePlay always discounts books by some percent. That's one form of sale.

Or if you have your book priced at $5.99 and put it through Bookbub for $2.99 for a short time, that's a discount.

And so on. Sales that lower a higher set price are called discounts.

The problem with starting your price of your book out so low in the first form, you have no room for the second part of discounting, and your main buyers are not necessarily loyal readers, but just discount buyers.

Pricing Your Book Because You Feel Insecure

Doing that is not a business strategy. That's a wake-up call that you need a confidence boost.

If you find yourself saying, "But I don't have a name so I should give my books away to get a name." You don't understand anything about this business.

And if you use the term, "I'm doing it to 'get readers,' you might want to really step back and look at your own reading habits.

Do you remember an author with one book that you stumbled upon and downloaded for free a year ago? And that author had nothing else at the time published. Do you honestly remember that author's name?

And if you downloaded it for free, did you even read it?

Building a fan base is one thing that is very real, and that comes over a lot of years and a lot of books. Put a newsletter sign-up on your website to see how many true fans you really have at the moment.

"Getting a reader" just doesn't work in any reality, especially when they didn't pay anything for the book.

Math for a Moment

Time to do a little math just for fun.

I am talking genre novels here. And I am only using Kindle pricing structure.

— Your Price… 99 cents. You get 35 cents per sale.
— Your Price… $1.99. You get 70 cents per sale.
— Your Price… $2.99. You get $2.09 per sale.
— Your Price… $3.99. You get $2.79 per sale.
— Your Price… $4.99. You get $3.49 per sale.
— Your Price… $5.99. You get $4.19 per sale.
— Your Price… $6.99. You get $4.89 per sale.
— Your Price… $7.99. You get $5.59 per sale.

Now I am a business person. I know a lot of writers are not, but I am, so my concern is finding a right mix of sales vs. price to get the largest income.

And this is where the fun comes in for every indie publisher.

Most of us know that the 99 cent and $1.99 price for novels is just too low for anything but a short term sale of a novel.

But look at that $2.99 price. You need to ask yourself this: If you set your price at $2.99, would you sell twice as many copies as you would sell at $5.99 to make basically the same amount of money?

And would that sales rate sustain?

That's a decent business question and I honestly have no answer because, as I said above. It depends.

FOR ME PERSONALLY, I would like the $5.99 rate because it allows me to do sales along the way. I also like the $7.99 price because every sale makes a lot of nice income. And it looks better when discounted as well.

And I can bundle them, lowering the price per book down and still make great money.

And my books look close enough to traditional published prices as to not shout that they are not. I like having my books lumped in that area, just under the prices of traditional publishers. My books, in comparison, look like a deal compared to a $9.99 electronic book from Putnam.

But not a devalued deal.

But that's just me personally. As a business person, I like the upper three prices for the reasons I stated and a number more. But again, there are no right answers.

But if you don't look at that math when making the decision, chances are you are making a wrong decision for the wrong reasons.

This is a business. You have a product to sell. Each product is unique, so make the pricing decision on that, not on some myth belief that indie books must be priced low.

What about Short Fiction Pricing?

I personally price my short stories at $2.99 and then do a paper edition for the stand-alone story and price it at $4.99.

Do I expect many people to buy a short story in paper for $4.99? No, but I like them and am using them for other things, such as signed paper bundles and so on.

But the $4.99 price for a paper edition of the short story makes the $2.99 look better to the consumer and I do sell short stories at that price. Not a great deal, but some.

Would I sell more at 99 cents? Sure. Would I make more money with my short stories priced at 99 cents? Probably not.

For every story I sell, I get $2.09 cents at $2.99. I would get 35 cents at 99 cents. I would need six sales at 99 cents to make about the same amount as selling one at $2.99. I can't see that happening with short stories.

Plus, my stories are worth $2.99.

And to hold off a bunch of questions, that price is for anything under 10,000 words. Anything. I trust my readers to know if they want to have an experience for $2.99 or not. That's up to them.

Again, no right answer.

The freedom of indie publishing means you can set your own price for your own reasons.

But I suggest you look at real business reasons for each pricing choice.

Collections and Bundles?

I tend to price collections electronically around the same price as a novel, maybe a little less. (Right now I am in the process of redoing my few collections and doing a bunch more.) On bundles, it flat depends. No set answer at all.

Now interestingly enough, I do *Smith's Monthly*, an 80,000 word "collection" magazine every month with a full novel in it, four or five short stories, some nonfiction, and two serial novels.

I sell that electronically for less than what I sell the novel for when the novel comes out as a stand-alone a few months later. My fans are slowly picking up on that and subscribing to the *Monthly*, which gets them an even better deal.

That's my way.

Smith's Monthly is good value for content and price. My short stories are set where I am comfortable and they sell a few, my novels I set in the price range just under traditional, but not much.

Those are my business choices. And what is great fun, I get to make the choices.

And so do you.

Genre Does Matter

No discussion of pricing in this moment in time would be even close to complete without mentioning genre.

Electronic books are major factors now in many genres, even though across all of publishing electronic books are around the 23% level of all book sales. But in some genres, that number has soared past 50% and is still climbing. And in erotica, it might be approaching 100% for all I know.

So with your pricing business decisions, you must be aware of your genre. For example, many, many readers in romance are near discount readers. They are rabid readers who can devour three or four books per day without an issue. So price is critical to them.

And romance writers have always been fast writers, but now even they have had to pick up speed to keep their readers satisfied. So if you are writing into the romance or erotica genres, you would be better served to price down in the $2.99 to $3.99 area.

On the other side of the coin, mystery and thriller readers are paper readers, and high value readers. Electronic sales are not large yet in the mystery genre.

Mystery readers will spend $8.99 for a mass market paperback or $27.99 for a hardback. There are very, very few discount mystery readers, so you would be better served to shout to the mystery readers that your books have value electronically and get the price in the $6.99 to $7.99 range. And make sure you have a paper edition as well.

Genre plays into your business decisions on pricing. Never forget that.

Summary

Pricing for indie publishers has settled into a range from $2.99 to $7.99 for electronic novels. Depending on a host of factors.

Every publisher, every author, needs to decide for themselves how they want to present themselves to readers.

Every publisher needs to understand the reality of their own genre.

So my suggestions to you to help you find your right price for a book:

1... Look at your genre and the pricing of the other books in that genre. Both traditional and indie.

2... Start your book slightly higher than you feel is right. You can do sales to give readers deals.

3... Take a long approach. Put your book up at a price and go back to writing. Check the income and sales per month, but don't touch the price (except for a special sale like a Bookbub) for one year. (See Chapter Six on Giving Your Garden Time to Grow.)

4... When you have four or five books in a series, but not before, think about discounting the first one down some (but not too low) to draw in readers. And do sales and special promotions on that first book to get readers into the series. That's the time you can start using price as a really effective weapon in sales.

5... Watch what the traditional publishers are doing for electronic books in your genre at least once per year and stay just below them. That will make your book look professional, yet give readers a deal. Again, a long-term effective way to use the power of price.

6... Get a long-term business plan and stick with it. And by long term, I mean at least five years or more. At least. And most of that plan should be focused on writing, not pricing.

Every indie publisher now has the choice of what to price their own books. Every indie publisher is different.

Base your pricing decisions on a business plan, set the price on a book, and forget it for a year before looking at the price decision again. (Except for sales.)

This choice is a wonderful thing we now all have.

But don't let the choice drive you away from your writing.

Set it, forget it.

Go have fun writing the next book.

Sacred Cow #10

THERE IS ONLY ONE WAY
TO PUBLISH A BOOK

This myth is so flat wrong, it's funny. Yet you hear writers arguing and getting angry at other writers because the other writer is not doing something "right," as if there is a "right" or "wrong" way.

Nope.

The right way is your way, the way that makes you happy, makes you money.

Some History

Almost from the beginning of indie publishing, bloggers, me included, were giving our opinions of this new world. And we all gave suggestions with our opinions. Joe Konrath, Barry Eisler, Kristine Kathryn Rusch, and I all are from traditional publishing and our opinions, good or bad, at first were colored by our experiences living for decades in that traditional system.

Some of what we suggested was right, some got dated quickly. I still think the best book written on this freelance lifestyle for indie writers was by Kris called **The Freelancer's Survival Guide.**

And what Joe and Barry have done over the years to keep all of us headed in decent directions has been stunning. And now Hugh Howey and Data Guy, along with The Passive Guy, are flowing information to all of us so fast, it's sometimes hard to keep up.

As this publishing world has expanded for writers, so have the options and the ways of making great money in this publishing business.

In traditional publishing, the road was set for you. Write a lot and get better and submit until you got an agent who then could help you sell books.

When I came in ahead of the agent-control phase, the path was write a lot, meet editors at conferences, sell your books to them, have your agent fetch the coffee and chase the money.

That was the path. Simple and clear.

Now the path is not simple and it is far, far from clear.

And anyone who tells you there is only one way to do something now in publishing just hasn't got their head up out of the sand. Or they just time-traveled from the last century forward.

Some Options

Option #1… Do everything yourself.

This option is how many of us started working on the indie side, and many still do. The writer does everything himself, from covers to blurbs to trading with friends for proofing. The writer puts the books on the bookstore sites, promotes what they can, and goes back to writing.

What is nice about this method to start is the learning curve is steep, yes, but it is possible. And all the money is yours that comes in.

There is very, very little real set costs with this method. Some art, maybe a business license, that's it. The time to write the book is the biggest overall cost.

I tend to suggest all writers start this way with their indie publishing business because it teaches you many things about the publishing business.

Option #2... Hire Some Stuff Done.

This option works well for those who don't feel they can do their own covers, or who don't want to tackle the chore of doing epubs and getting things launched on different sites.

At a certain point, almost all writers hire at least a good co-pyeditor. That's critical.

This option, in theory, gives you more time to write, but in the long run, really doesn't. You are spending time making sure things are done, often more time than if you learned how to do the task yourself.

Another downside on this option is the upfront costs. This limits your ability to write a lot of things like I am doing.

The good side is you don't have the learning curve of knowing what makes a great cover. The bad side is that you don't have that learning curve as to know what makes a great cover, so your sales are dependent on someone else's ideas of a good cover. That is always dangerous.

Option #3... You only write, hire everything else.

This option is used by many, many traditional writers who are working to get their backlist up and write new books at the same time.

This option is done in two ways.

One way is to hire a company like Lucky Bat Books and see if they will take and do your book for you. They do the copy-editing, professional covers, lay everything out, and set up the accounts for you. All for a fee and you get all the money.

This option is great for a slower writer who only does a book a year or so. Retired age writers do this a great deal and it's a great choice.

The other way is the way Kris and I did it. I started off (after my traditional years) in **Option #1**, letting the money build up, then we slowly started hiring help as the money increased, and now, except for my magazine, *Smith's Monthly*, we have full-time employees building a business that publishes our books and stories, among other projects.

Option #4... Sell Your Book to a Small Press.

This has some good and bad points to it, and everything depends on the contract you sign. If they can't pay you anything up front, caution. They may be offering a good royalty split, but chances are you might not see your half of the split if the owner of the small press needs to pay a house payment that month.

Small presses always depend on who is in charge. Watch your contract, be able to get out quick.

But the nice thing is that they do the work for you at their cost. The bad thing is that they might put a really ugly cover on your book and keep your money.

It's an option, but caution, some of the great horror stories come from writers who went to small presses.

Option #5... Sell Your Book to Traditional Publishing.

This is a very long and slow process now, with a lot of issues with it. It might take four or five years to get your book into print, and that's if it fits some unknown publishing vision of an editor and you are lucky.

From agents to bad contracts to bad editing, traditional publishing isn't a path I would suggest until things level out.

Many traditional companies are going to be in financial hurt and shutting down entire imprints and merging and laying off editors over the next few years. It's a mine field you would have to be scary lucky to make it through.

Remember, I published over 100 books with traditional publishers and this new world of traditional publishing flat scares me. I'd rather go play poker again than sell a book back into that mess. But that's just my opinion. Make your own decision.

Option #6… Have Your Agent Publish Your Books for You.

This again is full of all sorts of issues, including money issues. Your agent has suddenly become a publisher and is collecting money on your sales, money you can't account for because your agent gets it all first, and then takes a cut and sends you the rest. You can only hope it's the right amount.

Plus agents have fifty clients they are doing this for, so your book will get no attention. And chances are they are hiring out most jobs as well. I don't see this option being around for more than another ten years max as agencies collapse under the weight and lack of money. They will take your money with them when they go down. That is a proven fact in just the last year.

Option #7… Brand New Forms of Publishing Businesses.

This is part of the fun of this new world. I've seen numbers of new forms of publishing starting up. Authors grouping together to share skills, forming a co-op of sorts. Authors grouping together to form publishing companies like Kris and I have done to get more clout in promotion and sales and distribution.

The key with this path is be careful and watch who has control of the money.

Option #8, 9, and so on… Who knows what will be invented or is blooming right now for options for writers.

So many new things are coming along, the best thing we can all do is keep our eyes open and be willing to take a look at a new option when it opens up. It's a wonderful new world.

Caution on the scam publishers out there.

Every traditional publishing company now has a pay-to-play publishing imprint or two or three imprints, that are similar to the old vanity press scams of ten years ago. I don't consider those an option and I hope no one reading this does either.

The Harm of this Myth

The sad thing about this myth of believing there is only one way is that it doesn't just apply to indie publishers, but to all writers. In fact, this myth is chanted the loudest to the young writers coming in that think that there is only one way: Get an agent, sell a book.

Get an agent, sell a book.

Get an agent, sell a book.

Get an agent, sell a book.

It's like a bad nightmare.

Nope, it is far from the only way to get your book to readers who will love it.

Another area of harm is when this myth invades a writer's writing mind.

The writer starts thinking that the only way to make it is have fifty books and the writer must write a dozen books a year and work a day job and have family time with kids.

Well, gang, you watch me write a novel a month on my Writing in Public blog, but remember, I've been doing this for almost forty years. And I write short novels, seldom over 50,000 words long. And I live with another writer and we have no children.

In my first few years of writing seriously, I was excited I managed a short story per week. If I had been able to watch a Silverberg or a Resnick writing at my pace now (They did, and faster), I would have been stunned that it was even possible, and if I had tried it back then, I would have been frustrated and just quit. That's the truth.

So don't let anyone tell you there is only one way to produce words. There is your way. I would suggest that if you are writing a certain way and only producing one novel every year, you may want to explore other ways until you find something that helps you pick up speed.

But if you don't want to pick up speed, then don't. No right way, only your way.

You Must Write (blank) to Make a Living

Holy crap, any time you hear anyone say that, just laugh in his or her face. Or let me know and I'll laugh at them.

That is flat the dumbest advice and the most harmful advice anyone could ever give.

And if you hear yourself thinking that you should move to (blank) genre to make more sales, laugh at yourself.

Folks, the best way to get to riches with your writing is flat be an artist. Protect your work, write what makes you passionate, what you love, what makes you angry, or as Stephen King says, what scares you.

Write to passion.

Never write to market.

Who knows, maybe what you are writing will be the next hot things and you will look like a genius for being out ahead of all the followers.

Summary

In this modern world of publishing, there is no one way, no right way, no perfect path.

My suggestion is to keep your eyes open on the publishing side, look around, try one way or another, and be willing to change if something sounds right.

Do a writing plan and a business plan as to where you want to be in five years and figure out if the plan is realistic for your writing.

Write to passion.

And never listen to anyone who tells you there is only one right way.

There is only your way.

Experiment, learn, find it, and have fun.

ABOUT THE AUTHOR

USA Today bestselling writer Dean Wesley Smith published more than a hundred novels in thirty years and hundreds of short stories across many genres.

He wrote a couple dozen *Star Trek* novels, the only two original *Men in Black* novels, Spider-Man and X-Men novels, plus novels set in gaming and television worlds. He wrote novels under dozens of pen names in the worlds of comic books and movies, including novelizations of a dozen films, from *The Final Fantasy* to *Steel* to *Rundown*.

He now writes his own original fiction under just the one name, Dean Wesley Smith. In addition to his upcoming novel releases, his monthly magazine called *Smith's Monthly* premiered October 1, 2013, filled entirely with his original novels and stories.

Dean also worked as an editor and publisher, first at Pulphouse Publishing, then for *VB Tech Journal,* then for Pocket Books. He now plays a role as an executive editor for the original anthology series *Fiction River.*

For more information go to www.deanwesleysmith.com, www.smithsmonthly.com or www.fictionriver.com.

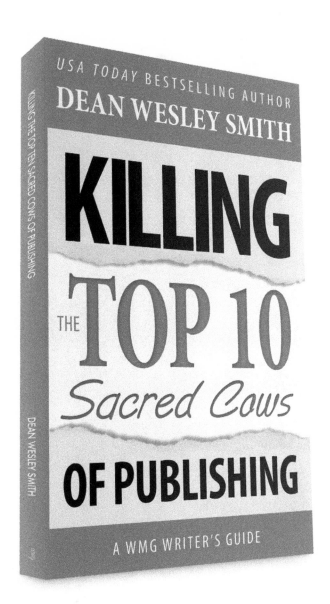

USA TODAY BESTSELLING AUTHOR

DEAN WESLEY SMITH

KILLING

THE TOP 10 *Sacred Cows*

OF PUBLISHING

A WMG WRITER'S GUIDE

Want to see Dean debunk more myths of publishing?
Try the companion book to this one, *Killing the Top
Ten Sacred Cows of Publishing,* on sale now.

CPSIA information can be obtained
at www.ICGtesting.com
Printed in the USA
LVHW04s1958040718
582656LV00001B/52/P